A note from The **SUPER** Lettering Book team ...

If you are reading this book, you are probably **EXCELLENT** at writing an ordinary alphabet. Good work!

Every school day, kids like you spend **HOURS and HOURS and HOURS** writing perfect letters, words, and sentences.

Think you know it all? **THINK AGAIN!**

This book is about drawing—or "lettering"—alphabets that are:

FANCY, and

INSANELY CRAZY FANCY

This isn't just any old lettering book, this is ...

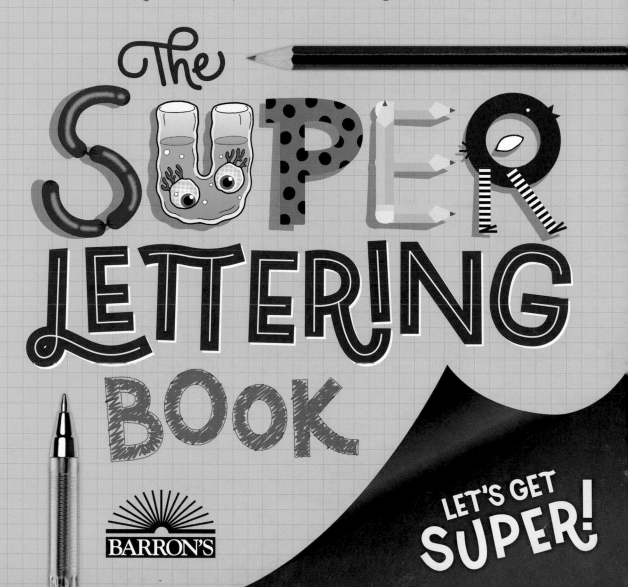

The **SUPER LETTERING BOOK**

BARRON'S

LET'S GET SUPER!

The Super Lettering Book is full of inspiring tips on how to create alphabets and words that will make your eyes **POP**.

Not so long ago, the super lettering artists in this book were kids who loved doodling—just like **You**! With practice, you might become a professional doodler, too! How cool is that?

At first, you might trace the trickier alphabets and words in this book. That is a great way to explore how letters are formed. Soon, you'll be creating your own alphabets and words.

Happy lettering!

SAMONE

The Super Lettering Book editor

hello

LETTERING TOOL KITS

You probably have a basic lettering tool kit already. Dig around in your pencil case and see what you can find.

PAPER

RULER

BASIC LETTERING TOOL KIT

ERASER

SHARPENER

PENCILS

30 29 28 27 26 25 24 23 22 21

Pens range from very thin to super thick.

Thin line

A

Thick line

Experiment with thick pens and thin pens when drawing your letters.

SUPER LETTERING TOOL KIT

If you want to get fancy, add these things to your tool kit:

- ☐ ballpoint pens
- ☐ felt-tip pens
- ☐ fountain pens
- ☐ glitter pens
- ☐ highlighter pens
- ☐ pencils
- ☐ crayons
- ☐ chalk
- ☐ paint
- ☐ scissors
- ☐ scrap paper
- ☐ graph paper
- ☐ tracing paper
- ☐ compass
- ☐ feather quill and ink (like Shakespeare— who knows, maybe he wrote his plays in crazy lettering!)
- ☐ dirt and a stick

PLAN YOUR WORK

It is important to carefully plan your work. Imagine you are doing a school project about weather. Here are some steps on how you might draw the word WEATHER in interesting letters.

Step 1: BRAINSTORM

A "brainstorm" is a funny way to describe writing all your ideas in one spot. Start by writing the word "WEATHER" in the center of a page. Then, write all the weather-related words that jump into your head (use arrows pointing out from the word WEATHER).

WEATHER

thermometer

sun hat

sunshine

summer
beach
swimming

wind

clouds

autumn
leaves
golden

seasons

spring
grow
flowers

winter
skiing
snowman

meteorologist

hot

forecast

cold

mild

rain

boots

storm

umbrella

wet

thunder

rainbow

dry

jungle

lightning

puddles

desert

snow

TIPS

Your brainstorm doesn't have to be neat!

Step 2: SKETCH

Next, study your brainstorm. Do these words give clues to how you might want to letter the word WEATHER? Start by sketching in pencil and build on your best ideas like this:

Brainstorm, sketch, and polish these words:

tennis match
ballet dancer
swimming pool
dog walker
cat nap

Step 3: POLISH

Choose your favorite sketch. Color it in, add highlights, patterns, and textures, and create dark outlines in pen.

5

ADD DIMENSION

Do you want your letters to really POP? Try adding drop lines, drop shadows, or drop shades. These give your work a cool three-dimensional look.

Here's how you do it:

Drop line →

Drop shadow →

Drop shade →

Step 1: IMAGINE A LAMP

Imagine a lamp is sitting on your page. Draw a tiny dot to represent where the lamp is sitting.

Tiny dot ↘

GLOW

Step 2: IMAGINE BEAMS OF LIGHT

Imagine the lamp is shining light on your letters. Your drop line, drop shadow, or drop shade should be drawn on the opposite side of your letters and the lamp. Play around with the lamp's position.

GLOW

Drop line ↗

GLOW

Drop shadow →

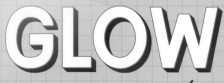

GLOW

Drop shade ↗

RULE GUIDELINES

If you want your lettering to sit neatly, you need to rule guidelines in gray pencil. Always rule your guidelines lightly and carefully erase them later.

TIPS 💡

Instead of measuring spaces between your letters, just look at them and judge how much space you need. Some letters look better bunched up or overlapping, while other letters need big gaps!

Step 1: RULE THREE LINES

hello

These three lines will show you where your big and small letters should sit.

Try using a compass for curved letters.

rainbow

Step 2: RULE A FOURTH LINE

goodbye

This fourth line will show you where the tails on lowercase letters like "g" or "p" should sit.

Step 3: ADD DIAGONAL LINES

If you are drawing slanting letters, diagonal lines will keep them on the same lean.

😄 LET'S START LETTERING!

Going Places

This paper-cut alphabet is simple, fun, and can be done on the run! Each letter has a choppy "freestyle" look to create a feeling of movement.

Letters shouldn't be perfect.

A B C D E F G H I J

No round edges here!

K L M N O P Q R S

Slanted letters look like they are going somewhere FAST…

T U V W X Y Z

TIPS

For a true paper-cut alphabet, use scissors to cut bright paper scraps into letters. Try cutting up old postcards or travel photos.

Look in travel guidebooks for inspiration.

SEE! 🌐
TRAVEL! 👀
EXPLORE!

Short words look great in this bold paper-cut style!

Try drawing a lowercase alphabet.

Let's Experiment

Think about what you want to letter. Is it the name of a famous landmark? Is it the name of a big city or somewhere in the wilderness? Is this place hot or cold?

ACROPOLIS

Yellowstone

Niagara Falls

SYDNEY OPERA HOUSE

EASTER ISLAND

STONEHENGE

Where have you visited? Where would you like to go?

Try lettering these words:

New York City

The Amazon

Mount Everest

Pyramids of Giza

Hawaii

Great Barrier Reef

Disney World

Tower of London

Great Wall of China

Angkor Wat

Eiffel Tower

SUPER LETTERING ARTIST

GEORGIA PERRY

Things that inspire me: Visiting new countries, watching movies, and hanging out with my friends!

Top tip to young letterers: Don't ever stop drawing! Look around at the letters, words, and signs you see in the world—soak them up like a sponge and then turn them into something new!

ULURU

TOWER OF PISA

Mount Fuji

HOLLYWOOD

Taj Mahal

11

Cool 4 School

This swirly alphabet is seriously fancy. If you have received a special award or certificate at school, you might have seen script lettering just like this!

Start with an outline of your letter.

Fill it in with your chosen shade.

Add highlights to the body of the letter.

Add contrasting highlights outside of the letter. Now it really pops!

TIPS

Experiment with pens and pencils. A brush can add smooth flourishes, while a fine-point pen is perfect for highlights.

SSSUPER!

Try drawing a lowercase alphabet.

abc

Draw your own fun stamps to reward your hard work!

GOOD WORK!

TOP OF THE CLASS!

Bee your BEST!

study

homework

Try lettering more words like these ...

Let's Experiment

Think about subjects you study at school. What tools help you to write an essay or solve an equation? Experiment with words you use in science class like "experiment!"

periodic table

computer

ESSAY

beaker

writing

What other words remind you of school?

Try lettering these words:

school bus

grades

uniform

teacher's pet

history

world map

library

sports

blackboard

students

atom

microscope

SUPER LETTERING ARTIST

KATE PULLEN

Things that inspire me: So many things spark little moments of creativity. Music, books, friends, movies, food . . . even my small patch of garden.

Top tip to young letterers: Your sketches don't have to be perfect; it's just about putting pen to paper.

BOOKWORM

MATHEMATICAL GENIUS

bacteria

Celebrate

This playful alphabet seems to dance like a conga line of letters. Drop shadows matched with angled letters help it "move" across the page. The crazy patterns look like a smashed piñata!

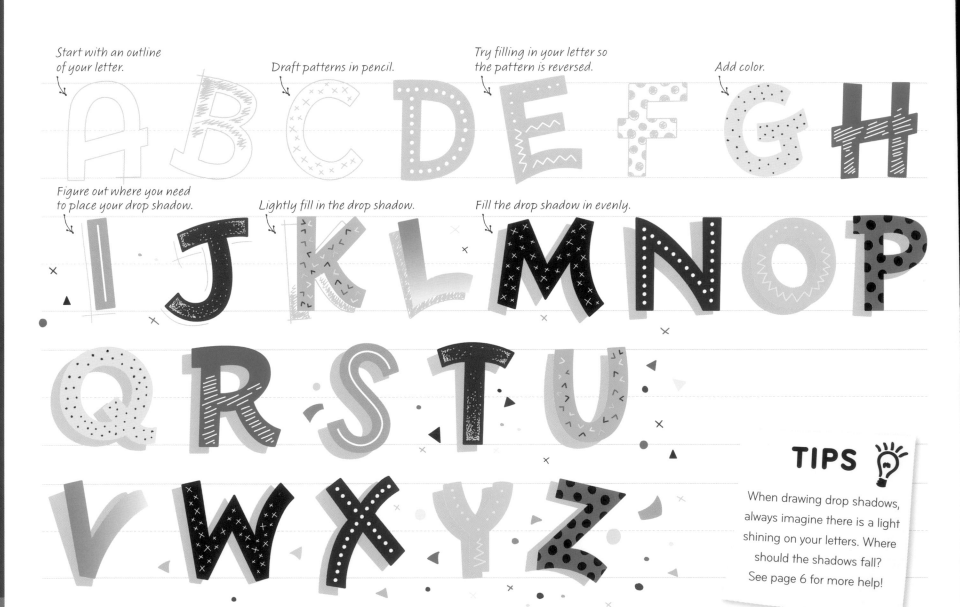

Start with an outline of your letter.

Draft patterns in pencil.

Try filling in your letter so the pattern is reversed.

Add color.

Figure out where you need to place your drop shadow.

Lightly fill in the drop shadow.

Fill the drop shadow in evenly.

TIPS

When drawing drop shadows, always imagine there is a light shining on your letters. Where should the shadows fall? See page 6 for more help!

Try lettering a lowercase alphabet.

abc

PARTY ON, DUDES!

FUN

TUNES

Guidelines help your work look polished. See how these letters are spaced evenly across the curve?

Try lettering more words.

Let's Experiment

How do you celebrate special occasions with your family and friends? Think about the things you do and the words you say. These words are perfect for creating your own party invitations and greeting cards!

birthday cake

HAPPY NEW YEAR!

HOORAY!

SURPRISE!

Valentine's Day

gifts

There is always something worth celebrating!

Try lettering these words:

streamers

disco ball

party animal

musical chairs

wedding bells

dance floor

pin the tail on the donkey

tuxedo

ball gown

party hats

piñata

SUPER LETTERING ARTIST

ELIZA SVIKULIS

Things that inspire me: Painted signs, food packaging, and very old books.

Top tip to young letterers: Create your own collection of lettering references in a big folder or box. Keep food labels with fancy logos and cut out ads with wacky lettering!

Fireworks

BALLOONS

dance off!

confetti

good times!

Creatures

Feathers, fur, scales, and spikes form this creepy-crawly alphabet. Some of the letters explore how a creature moves, while other letters emphasize quirky details!

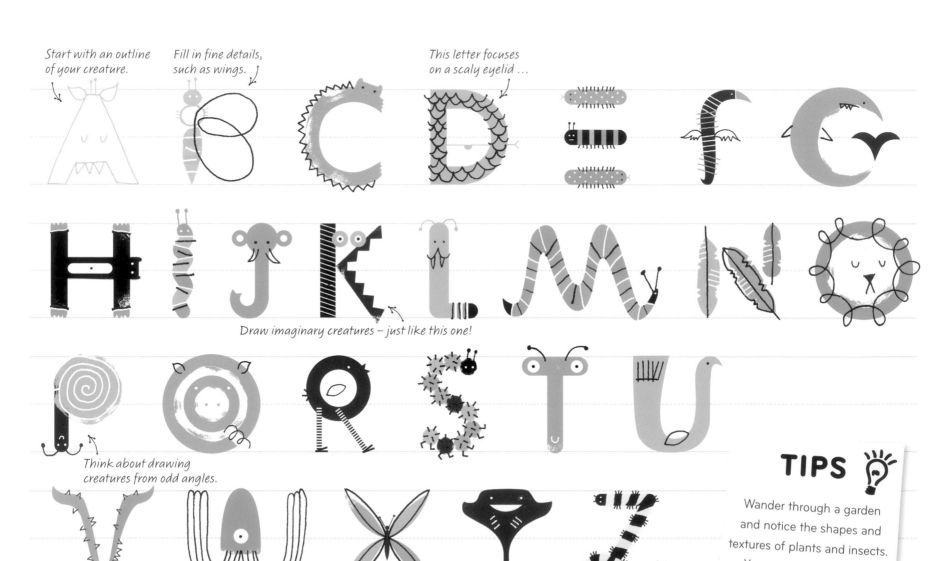

Start with an outline of your creature.

Fill in fine details, such as wings.

This letter focuses on a scaly eyelid ...

Draw imaginary creatures – just like this one!

Think about drawing creatures from odd angles.

When in doubt, add some spikes.

TIPS

Wander through a garden and notice the shapes and textures of plants and insects. You might find lettering inspiration digging in the dirt!

Try lettering more words.

You could try drawing a tiny snail or beetle here …

CUTE
CUDDLY
FIERCE

Try lettering a lowercase alphabet.

Let's Experiment

Animal and insect words are fun to draw. Does your
creature live in a reef or in the jungle? Does it howl or
growl? Does it have whiskers, fangs, or stripes?
Does your creature even exist?

*Try lettering
these words:*

log

wormhole

caterpillar

wings

tadpole

desert

firefly

dolphin

paw prints

ocean

*Think about
animals and the
places they live ...*

ants

SUPER LETTERING ARTIST
★ MICHELLE MACKINTOSH ★

Things that inspire me: Traveling, nature, animals, and finding everyday objects that hold enormous beauty.

Top tip to young letterers: See if you can find patterns or shapes in your letters that relate directly to your words. You could add tails, horns, or paws to lettering about animals or draw letters in the shape of the creature.

forest

Fangs

fins

Butterfly

slither

23

Street Art

Look around any town or city and you will spy inspiring street art in alleys and public spaces. This alphabet bounces from the page with chunky letters, subtle shading, and "3D" shadows.

Sketch in pencil first.

Add color. The artist has blended yellow, pink, orange, and a touch of blue.

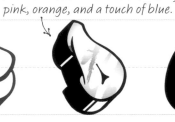

The dot is joined to the body of the I.

The drop shadows have shiny highlights.

These letters are SERIOUSLY puffy, but keep their original form!

TIPS

When drawing a new alphabet, make sure your letter shapes look like they belong together. Try to match the way letters lean or the colors you use.

Play around with colors and blending.

Street art is sometimes tricky to read ... that's what makes it SUPER COOL!

Try overlapping your letters and drawing one big drop shadow.

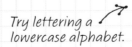

Try lettering a lowercase alphabet.

25

Let's Experiment

Street art is usually big and loud! Sometimes it seems to shout from the walls. What is your message? Is it love and good vibes? Are you thinking blah blah blah? Do you just want to say hi?

Give yourself a funny nickname and try lettering it!

Try lettering these words:

peace out!

awesome

happiness

graffiti

magic happens!

spray paint

daydreamer

wise guy

cooooooooool

airbrush

SUPER LETTERING ARTIST

GEORGE ROSE

Things that inspire me: Talking! I love bouncing ideas off other creative people and starting discussions about their processes.

Top tip to young letterers: Use unexpected tools to create your letter shapes—the more experimental the better. Try brooms instead of brushes, tie sticks together to create 3D type, paint on a balloon instead of paper!

Snack Time

It's always snack time with this delicious, food-themed alphabet. Fruits and vegetables mix with fast food treats to form a banquet of letters. Are you hungry yet?

This wedge of watermelon is definitely an A shape ...

Chopsticks help the noodles become an F.

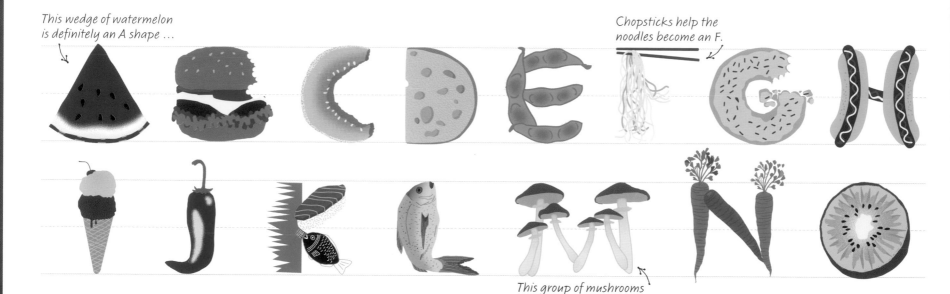

This group of mushrooms form the perfect M.

Some foods naturally go together ...

A bite turns this pizza slice into a V.

TIPS

Create letters with real food on your plate. Shape cooked rice or mashed potatoes into fluffy, cloud-like letters!

BREAKFAST!
LUNCH!
DINNER!
YUMMY!

These round foods are perfect for punctuation marks.

Experiment with cutlery!

EAT

Let's Experiment

You have probably been playing with food since you were a baby! Think about shapes, colors, patterns, and textures. Foods can be sliced, diced, stacked, and mixed. Sauces and mustards are perfect for swirly lettering!

Is your favorite food listed here? If not, try lettering it!

Try lettering these words:

pretzels

apple pie

milkshake

orange juice

chocolate

jelly beans

salad

cheese

cookies

pancakes

ice cream

FRENCH FRIES

SUPER LETTERING ARTIST

ALICE OEHR

Things that inspire me: Cooking, art galleries, travel, my friends, and my cat.

Top tip to young letterers: Don't worry about trying to make your letters look like a real font. Go crazy and have fun! Experiment with drawing letters using things from real life. Just make sure your crazy, fun letters can be clearly understood!

PIZZA

FRUIT SALAD

TACO

SPICY

Creepy Stuff

This alphabet is seriously creepy, kooky, and super-duper spooky. The letters are inspired by haunted houses, mad scientists, and ghost stories to make your skin crawl!

Brains make the perfect B.

Green makes spooky stuff look gross!

This caterpillar with pincers makes an angry J.

Eyeballs in a jar for U? Eeeeeew!

     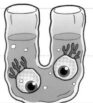 

TIPS

When drawing spooky letters, always wait until after dark! Hide under your blanket and use a flashlight to light up the page. WARNING: Don't get too freaked out!

Try lettering a lowercase alphabet that drips ...

EEEK!

GOOSEBUMPS!

SPOOKY...

Play around with shapes. This bloodthirsty shark makes an awesome A.

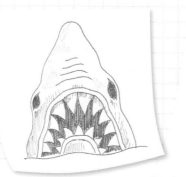

Think about creepy ways to draw exclamation marks!

Let's Experiment

Open the creakiest door in your imagination and see what you find! Is it covered in spider webs? Does a black cat cross your path? Maybe your imagination is full of SLUDGE!

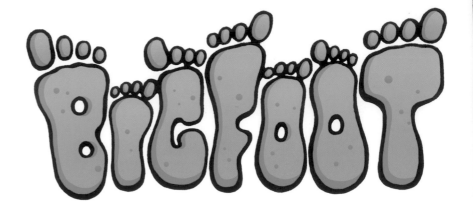

Do any of these words make your hair stand on end?

Try lettering these words:

midnight

zombies

dungeon

vampire

spiders

bats

Friday the 13th

mad scientist

cauldron

Jack-o-lantern

SUPER LETTERING ARTIST

WHAT_THE_HELLO (BENJAMIN JOHNSON)

Things that inspire me: Music, art, fashion, and creepy old cartoons! In the 1930s, almost all cartoons looked creepy!

Top tip to young letterers: A good way to find your own style is to imagine a world where your letters and drawings live! Think about your crazy world every time you sit down to draw something new.

Outer Space

This futuristic, space-themed alphabet uses stripes and sharp angles to create a 3D look. Different shades of blue work together to give the letters a metal-like shine.

Start by sketching the outline of your letters.

Sketch some internal lines to give a raised effect.

Add your chosen colors.

Draw in some lines to finish off your letters.

Different shades of blue create a shiny appearance.

Narrow lines give the letters depth.

TIPS

Stripes and clever shading can give your letters a chiseled 3D look that really zooms from the page!

Try lettering other words.

UFO

SPACE.
IT'S OUT THERE.

Add decorative elements. Stars and starbursts look super cosmic.

STARS

Letter a lowercase alphabet.

abc

Let's Experiment

The cosmos has infinite worlds and words to letter!
Think about spaceships, planets, and other galaxies.
Do you ever wonder if there is life on Mars? What
would Martian lettering look like?

*Gaze at the night
sky for inspiration!*

**Try lettering
these words:**

The Solar System

asteroid

satellite

shooting star

supernova

UFO

black hole

light years

The Big Bang

Mission Control

eclipse

Things that inspire me: Ideas can come from anywhere and everywhere: billboards, magazines, street graffiti, old book engravings, and historic calligraphy.

Top tip to young letterers: Research! Get inspired by different lettering styles and experiment with different ways to represent your letter shapes.

astronaut

nebula

orbit

planets

ALiENS?

STENCILS AND BONUS WORDS

Use the stencils and bonus words on the following pages to create cool cards, posters, and signs!

BEWARE DOG

EPIC!

ballet

FLOWER CHILD

home sweet home

Letter a sign for your bedroom door!

Try lettering these words:

biohazard

SILENCE: GENIUS AT WORK

zombie sleeping

football star

tennis ace

SLAM DUNK!

sweet dreams